FATHER NA┼URE

Sabrina Nichole

Part I of II

FATHER NATURE

Copyright © 2024 by Sabrina Nichole.

Printed and bound in the United States of America

First edition

ISBN: 978-0-692-95777-6

In Loving Memory of

Carl Edward Ayers

Forever My Daddy

Sunrise: 11/16/1953

Sunset: 09/30/2020

Dedication

This book is dedicated to God – to include Jesus Christ and the Holy Spirit. I would also like to give tribute to my family, my friends, even my foes, whether real, counterfeit, or imagined. All have been a significant impact on my life's journey, and I appreciate the love, forgiveness, grace, support, compassion, knowledge, understanding, and encouragement provided over the years. I also [now] find value in tough times that challenged the very fiber of my being, such as the desolate seasons from which some of the following chapters were depicted.

Blessings, Love & Peace!

Yesterday, Today, Tomorrow; Forevermore.

~Sabrina Nichole

"*The beauty of nature is that it is always speaking —voicing a thought without words or sound and communicating emotion through mere illustration.*"

~*Sabrina Nichole*

Stages & Environments

I.   **INTRODUCTION**

II.   **THE BUTTERFLY STORY**

III. **THE CHAPTERS OF LIFE**
    a. The Beginning
    b. The Middle
    c. The End
    d. New Beginnings

IV. **THE SEASONS OF LIFE**
    a. Winter
    b. Spring
    c. Summer
    d. Fall

V.   **CLOSURE**
    a. Part I of II
    b. Letters to My Past

VI. **RECOMMENDED REFERENCES**
    a. The Names of God
    b. The Names of Jesus
    c. The Names of the Holy Spirit
    d. Other References

Introduction

The Ride

A lot of time has passed; nonetheless, I clearly remember how this book was birthed. I was riding the bus to work in the summer of 2003. I recall my initial plan to play music and enjoy not having to drive when I heard a still, small voice gently whisper, "*No music today. Sit back and enjoy the ride.*" I was quick to obey because I was desperate to hear what I called "The Voice of God."

As I rode the bus, I remember staring out the window in awe of God's creation: the beautiful blue sky with no clouds in sight, the sun shining so bright, the green grass glistening with iridescence alongside the highway, and birds flying freely, amongst the air's waves. It felt as if it was only me on the bus that day, yet all around me were cars clattering and people chattering amidst such internal serenity. I recall thinking to myself, "Lord, I feel You near," and as I pondered more of nature, I thought more and more of God, and then I started to write.

I remember asking the question, "Why do we call it 'Mother Nature' anyway?" Is it because mothers contain the womb that bears the seed of life? Is it because it's typically the nature of a woman to show signs of change more outwardly – comparable to seasons? Or is it because mothers tend to inherently nurture and protect her offspring?

As I meditated on this, it seemed as if my mind shifted to another dimension when suddenly, and ever so clearly, I thought of God as the all-time seed carrier of life. I also began to see the sun as the S-O-N, son, Jesus Christ, along with the air that we breathe as waves of His Spirit which often intertwines with Summer, Fall, Winter, and Spring. I was reminded about the importance of balance and the need for our spirit, soul, and body to be centered. The scriptures in Ecclesiastes 3 came to life in a whole new way for me this day:

"To everything, there is a season, and a time to every purpose under the heaven: a time to be born, and a time to die; a time to plant, and a time to pluck up that which is planted; a time to kill, and a time to heal; a time to break down, and a time to build up; a time to weep, and a time to laugh; a time to mourn, and a time to dance; a time to cast away stones, and a time to gather stones together; a time to embrace, and a time to refrain from embracing; a time to get, and a time to lose; a time to keep, and a time to cast away; a time to rend, and a time to sew; a time to keep silence, and a time to speak; a time to love, and a time to hate; a time of war, and a time of peace."

(KJV, verses 1-8)

Subsequently, as I pen the pages of this book, I seek both stability and the ability to surrender to God as I purpose to bring my mind, will, and emotions into subjection to His Spirit. I ask Him to heal and to reveal, to stir up hope and encouragement, to bring forth peace and enlightenment amid this humble effort to characterize what I attribute as being the nature of my Heavenly Father.

He is so loving, so patient, so kind. He is all-seeing, all-knowing, all-powerful, and ever-present. He is the very environment that I breathe, the very essence of life, justice, and liberty. He is a way-maker, a risk-taker, and I love Him with all of my heart; rather, if I am being honest, I'm trying to. But life keeps evolving, and I find myself doubting much more than I trust and hoping more, instead of standing in faith. I also admit to having a wandering mind at times, which is sometimes up, sometimes down, and sometimes up the street and around the corner while I'm washing dishes at my kitchen sink or, worse, at my neighbor's kitchen sink.

I believe such a conflict in one's mind is more common than not, no matter how many ways we may camouflage the battlefield. Accordingly, this book also aims to identify and illustrate some of the challenges we may endure in the process of rising above unhealthy conditions, both internally and externally.

It is not likely to be easy. In fact, at times it can be so excruciating that we feel convinced no one else understands.

As such, my prayer is that the readers and hearers of this book will be able to see beyond my disposition and instead sense, hear, and see attributes of God. May this book of seeds germinate the very depths of your soul and establish a root that grows deep for another to water but for God, in all His splendor and glory, to blossom and increase. In my eyes, He alone is worthy of any adoration or praise that may become of my efforts.

The Butterfly Story

I came across a narrative years ago called "The Butterfly Story." I absolutely loved the message of it and will attempt to paraphrase here:

There was a man who came across a cocoon. He stopped, stared, and eventually noticed a wing peering out. The man felt compelled to help, as bystanders often tend to do when they are near someone or something in need. He decided to split the entrance and exit way of the cocoon, also known as its covering. The butterfly was free! Or so it seemed. For it went thru life able to breathe, able to stand, able even to see; yet its' intended purpose – to fly – did not fully manifest. Why? Because butterflies must struggle out of their cocoon in order to gain the strength, endurance, and elasticity required to soar.

When I heard this depiction, something awakened on the inside of me. Over the years this feeling would only intensify, becoming the storyline of my various battles, and causing a series of questions I often turned to God to answer. Within this story, I also discovered what I call "the chapters of life," and I began to see with greater clarity that with every beginning, there is also a middle and an end. In alignment with this thought, I associated the beginning of life for the butterfly to a seed, an embryo, or even a thought, vision, or idea. As for the cocoon, I replaced it with words such as "holding place" or "womb" – be that underneath the surface or in one's mind; while I viewed the fluids within the cocoon simultaneous to nourishment, blood, or water.

Further, the time taken to develop from a caterpillar into a butterfly equated to the *'middle'* – a time of processing and preparation equivalent to a time of growth and initial manifestation of purpose. The middle is also critical because something or someone is being formed; yet, to fully develop, periods of discomfort and patience are often involved. This leads to the 'end' – a result I can best illustrate through the lens of a natural birth whereby outcomes range from healthy delivery to inconsistent growth or possibly even to no development at all. Inconceivably, such a result can also conclude with a fatality, but not necessarily a physical one; instead, it could be the death of spirit, the demise of hope, or the termination of a purpose that was meant to produce life.

As for the bystander, his actions appeared innocent, right? Or is it the contrary, with the interference more of a shadowing prerequisite to be more discerning when it comes to the purpose or position of struggle and willpower? "How or why is that?" one might ask. *Because sometimes the struggle is necessary to gain the wings needed to take flight.* Wings of strength and perseverance, wings that fuel purpose and survival, wings that give the ability to see beyond immediate circumstances and environments. For me, this involved observing beyond the pain of my today and yesterdays, to reflect with greater discretion for tomorrow.

To help illustrate this, imagine, if you will, an eagle soaring upon high. It can look above the head, eye level, or below; yet even for such a posture, there is always an area that cannot be seen, a level that is *always* a notch higher. We can look up and around to catch a glimpse of it, but we cannot be there and present at the same time. Such imagery is where I see the depth of God's wisdom and divine abilities. His thoughts are not our thoughts, and His ways are not our ways. Thus, as the following pages aims to depict, He is the God of initial purpose, vision, and creation, a distinction critically different from the aftermath of freewill choices. I, therefore, start this chapter both in recognition and in honor of Him, for I believe to know and understand such a role, one must go to the source of origin.

The Chapters of Life

The Beginning

Seed Carrier, Creator, God.

Merriam-Webster defines genesis as "the origin or coming into being of something." In the Holy Bible, the first book, or chapter, is called Genesis, and it is in this place I will attempt to define one of the many attributes of God - His nature as Creator. Further, to stay true to the word beginning, I will not go beyond the first four verses of section one, which reads:

¹In the beginning, God created heaven and the earth.

²And the earth was without form and void, and darkness *was* upon the face of the deep. And the Spirit of God moved upon the face of the waters.

³And God said, "Let there be light," and there was light.

⁴And God saw the light, that *it was* good: and God divided the light from the darkness.

(KJV, verses 1-4)

There are *four* concepts within these scriptures I would like to bring to the forefront. The *first* relates to the word 'beginning' and how, from the inception of the Bible, the fact that there was a *beginning* is referenced in the very first sentence of the very first chapter. I believe this demonstrates how God has a certain order of things. Furthermore, in conjunction with this beginning, there was also an end with an event that took place in between. Translation: You cannot start and end at the same time, no matter how short of a delay there is between transitions. Instead, there is generally a plan, an action, and a result, or to state another way, there is generally an occurrence, a reaction, and a solution.

The *second* concept pertains to how God created the Heavens and the Earth. I correlate this to being a necessary separation to establish order and eliminate confusion, for He did not launch a multitude of areas but two separate and distinct environments solely.

Third, the Bible states how the earth was "dark, without form and void." In other words, it had no true structure and was like a blank canvas before being placed in the hands of Picasso or *Armona Asianay* (my most beautiful, creative, and talented daughter). This means it existed, and it had potential, but there was emptiness. So, what did God do? *He painted!* —or, as the Bible puts it, He hovered.

Can you imagine with me, God moving and swaying (or dancing in some translations) as He began to make His mark on the earth? In doing so, He commanded light to come forth, which I relate to the need to know what is surrounding us, or why is it dark in the first place. This lesson has been invaluable to me over the years, and despite the poor choices I continue to sometimes make, I have since realized the only way I can learn certain things is to seek God's help. He freely gives awareness through His sight and lovingly shines a light on my blind spots. Then, He graciously guides me accordingly *whether I choose to follow Him or not.*

Last, the *fourth* concept. Once illumination was revealed, God applied His signature of approval and said, "This is good." A statement that has helped me to see how everything doesn't have to be in place immediately for something or someone to be considered right, or effective, especially when in the process of becoming. Instead, I believe God wants us to glean from these passages how He will complete us, along with the vision and purpose He has for and puts within us.

The subsequent scriptures explained how God continued to bring further order upon the earth, the manifestations of which remain today. In my opinion, this affirms we can trust God and that His words are true. After all, He is not like the friend, foe, family member, or lover that may have betrayed us, causing grief through falsehoods and other misconducts. Instead, He has our best interest at heart and genuinely accomplishes and sustains what He sets out to do. This includes self-preservation and healing if only we'd allow Him to hover over us, over our deepest voids and darkest places. The areas of emptiness and gloom in our lives. The places that contain no shape, no structure, no identity. He can change circumstances where the love affairs between our heart, spirit, and soul are in grave need of repair, for they have been adulterated, causing division to what was once a most beautiful union between peace and purity. He can heal the bonds of despair that are fastened by roots of varying issues and anxieties. He can help overcome the regions of defeat and victim mentalities.

Some may ask, "Why is God so willing to transform for the better, especially when shame from wrongdoings is a factor which has particularly made me feel unworthy?" Personally, I believe it's because He loves us too much to leave us in fragmented conditions. After all, He is considered our Heavenly Father, which means He is also a father to the fatherless. As such, He exudes wisdom and is a voice of reason whose correction and affection we can rely upon. On the other hand, and not too dis-similar to natural parenting, there is a stipulation if we desire the grace of His allowances, which involves not only giving God permission to intervene and guide us but also a willingness to obey what is instructed. During such times, there is a good chance we will not like all or some of what is required for change to take root and permeate; however, I have learned His process is indeed for our benefit and leads to total restoration and healing as opposed to counterfeit blessings.

Another thing I love about God is that He does not go against our freewill, yet His merciful nature covers and protects us without the weight of condemnation. There is a song that explains it this way, "If grace is an ocean, we are all sinking." To take this one step further, I think God wants an appreciation or love that is naturally developed and grows more and more over time, as opposed to a relationship built by force. At least, this has been my experience in connecting with Him for myself. For example, when I cried out to God from the aftermath of an impure development, instead of being manipulated or judged, a seed of hope was gently planted in my heart, which manifested into a relationship centered upon faith, clarity, trust, and unconditional love; as opposed to a connection stemming from fear, confusion and/or deceit.

The Power of Words (to include the unspoken word)

I must pause for a moment to reiterate the power of words. Have you ever had an experience where you said something you wished you could take back? Or perhaps something was said to or about you that still has a lasting effect. Often, this occurs when we fail to respond but instead react, especially when emotions or toxic cycles are involved.

An example of this is gleaned from a conversation I had with a very dear sister in Christ about fifteen years ago. She mentioned the slogan, "Sticks and stones may break my bones, but words will never hurt me." I remember her saying, "Broken bones can be mended," yet words that were spoken over her as a child still taunted her well into her adult years. Once I thought things over, I realized how I, too, suffered from words spoken about me. *This realization further illuminated how many of those words are from words I have spoken about me.* Such as when life began to get too heavy, and words such as "I'm tired" and "I don't think I'll ever make it out of this battle" became my daily language. In hindsight, I was so wounded and drained of being hurt that I began to focus on how I was feeling instead of on words and positive affirmations that would aid with my healing.

Let us ponder about the impacts of social media and music as another example. I am especially fond of music, and I often say that music and dance are my therapy. But with every good comes the potential for bad, and such modes of communication are no exception. Each have conveyed messages that tear down instead of build-up. Messages that give a negative identity or inflicts 'fear' as opposed to 'hope'. Messages that deceive, hinder, and shackle. Messages that stir up chaos and/or false accusations and images.

Plausibly, it stands to reason when a positive message is transmitted, it is more likely to manifest positive results. Thus, by speaking life into existence, I emphatically believe God not only demonstrated the power of words but provided a blueprint for a good foundation of the same. He furthered my belief by how He eliminated confusion and solidified order, establishing what I call the true *Master Plan*. One that rendered seed for growth and turned blemished perceptions into purpose.

A final thought centers upon the unspoken word and childhood experiences. I was six years old when my parents divorced. My siblings and I went to live with our mom, and when my dad and I would reunite next, I was sixteen. He was homeless at the time, and we didn't speak directly. At that moment I learned how loud and clear one can communicate merely with their eyes. So much was said, heard, and felt through our respective glares, and I stood there for what seemed to be hours gazing into his senses from a distance but hearing what he was exchanging as if we were talking in close proximity. I detected his love just as much as I felt the divine connection that will forever surpass and outweigh his absence in my life, which I hope was true for him in return.

On the other end of this spectrum were the unspoken expressions of my mom. As a single parent, she ensured her four children, and later her grandchildren always had the essentials needed (may God forever bless her heart and her efforts). She went to work every day and took great pride in the home-cooked meals she provided daily. I later realized my mom often hid her exhaustion when I discovered a book of her poems. I remember realizing how resilient she is and how I acquired so much from the example of her silent press despite times she camouflaged periods of unequivocal heartache and stress.

Let Us Pray:

Father God may the words of my mouth and the meditation of my heart be acceptable in thy sight, for You are my strength and my redeemer. I humbly ask for Your help to cast down every thought and imagining that is not of You. Thoughts of doubt. Thoughts of discouragement. Thoughts of defeat and distress. Thoughts centered upon words that cause chaos, confusion, and worry, derived from words that hide the message within the mess. In exchange, may You create in me a clean heart and renew my spirit righteously. And as You do, may You dig deep into my soul, dear Lord, to mend and repair not just the surface of my being but also the parts only You can see. May I be restored from every ache and anxious thought, being careful of what I speak both in private and in public. May You further bind and break every word, curse, and impure spirit from my bloodline along with the bloodline of all who and what I am connected to. And may You flood my soul and spirit in divine healing, peace, comfort and strength as only You can do.

The Chapters of Life

The Middle

The Cocoon, The Bearer/Receiver, Us.

Each section of this book is meant to be an interrelated continuum of my spiritual and soul crises at various stages of my life. I have endured – and continue to sometimes face – trials that may seem insignificant to others but have caused me a lot of grief and torment. There were breaks in between my struggles, but during this one season, I suffered seemingly without pause. The period lasted about three years, and I failed daily to abstain from my woes, worrying my loved ones constantly. I quickly learned I was nowhere near as strong as I thought I was, and my mistakes and failures began to choke more and more life out of me.

During this time, I grew desperate to relocate from my current state, and after dwelling in a negative bed of emotions and tarnished mindset for such an extended period, I began to consider a move to a different climate altogether. I thought if I could just change my literal environment, I would better enable myself to handle the issues that drowned my soul and heart. As tears engulfed my face, I heard a faint voice again, the same one that prompted the writings of this book. *"Changing your environment will not change you,"* the voice said so nonchalantly. In other words, what I was experiencing was not going to change merely because I relocated my external position. Instead, I needed to endure internal construction and was afraid because I knew feelings of shame, abandonment, rejection, and denial would be combated in the process. I also knew I would need to allow myself to feel in order to heal from the various layers of affliction and emotion, going through the pain, not around it, to include abstaining from temporary fixes.

Once I decided to yield to this journey, as opposed to delaying the need to endure it, as evidenced by the same dead ends manifested in different ways, I was led to study mourning, detoxification, and addiction. In doing so, I learned when in mourning, the stages we endure until healing manifests are the same, yet the length of time we remain in each phase varies immensely. Accordingly, while there is no set timetable for going through a grieving process, there are certain aspects we are sure to encounter, such as shock and denial, which, in my opinion, are a mechanism to 'cushion the blow' in a way our heart and mind can still function, albeit distressingly. The shakings of reality eventually awaken us to the realm of truth, and we resume an antagonizing passageway of sorrow. Thereafter, we start to feel the weight of turmoil more heavily as we crossover towards acceptance. After acceptance has developed more fully, we give room to hope, and it is here that we don't necessarily forget our pain, but instead, we may learn to forgive, let go, embrace lessons learned, and/or discover ways to cope, grow and move onward with our lives.

While studying addiction, I learned it consists of a brain disease that involves the craving of an unhealthy consumption that stimulates the need for a *fix*. One of the most eye-opening lessons on addiction is how this fix will continue to gain momentum until properly decontaminated, even when the *fix* results in life-threatening consequences and grave devastation to ourselves and/or the wellbeing of others.

When I researched detoxification, I learned it is two-fold. One method is a safe and supervised way to withdraw someone from an addiction, and the other is a more natural process of elimination whereby impurities are removed from the blood. If not properly filtered, the impure blood can affect every cell in the body. The first method of detoxification requires being under the care of a doctor, while the second approach can be done in the comfort of one's own home.

After I grasped a more thorough understanding of each focal area, I realized not only was I in mourning, I was also addicted and in need of detoxification. Further, it became clear that although a significant part of me died, the roots of who and what I mourned were still very much alive. I then sensed a need to confess and address head-on how my sickness may not have been from drugs or alcohol, two of the leading causes of addiction, but it was a disease, nonetheless. From that point forward, I was convinced illness and disease can occur from spiritual and soul wounds that require just as much, if not more, treatment to be restored to a healthy status. For instance, I was experiencing ailments similar to clogged arteries and cancerous cells and knew I desperately needed to heal not only my body but my mind, will, and emotions as well. Additionally, I noticed I had become addicted to flawed perceptions and behaviors that became crippling; and instead of applying pressure to the pain akin to physical therapy, I bandaged my wounds without treating the infection, which risked spread to other parts of me to include those connected to me.

I eventually decided to face what I was covering up, for I mastered the ability to hide behind a carefully crafted mask, outwardly displaying strength and composure yet inwardly falling deeper and deeper into graves of despair. I concluded as painful as it was to feel the weight of my dis-ease, it was a lot more dyer for me to ignore the spiritual and emotional surgery I needed. From a godly perspective, I believe I was suffering through trauma and afflictions only *thee* Master Physician could cure. Am I alone here? Or can you relate to sometimes being stuck in anguish that neither you nor any other physical entity can filter through, prescribe, or heal? I term this section the *middle* because this is where 'transition' occurs, and we must decide to go backward or forward, hold on or let go, stay put, or embrace the unknown. In doing so, we tend to only shift for the better when we confront the range of what is hindering us. This period generally takes the most time to maneuver through, along with a lot of patience and forgiveness of ourselves and others. It is an even longer duration when the infliction took a long time to cultivate, thus it is crucial to focus more on the root causes that may take some time to unfold, as opposed to on symptoms solely, which are sure to arise while in this state.

Let Us Pray:

Lord, I have grown so tired, weary and am in desperate need of repair. I heard You are the Master Physician, so I commit myself to Your care. I also heard You are the giver of wisdom; thus, I yield to Your instruction. After all, You are the creator of heaven and earth; so, who better to fix and restore my broken nature. Likewise, You are the giver of life; will You please breathe into me. For I feel like I am suffocating and heard You are strong when I am weak. You are all-seeing, all-knowing, ever-present, and all-powerful; what is impossible with man is possible with You. Accordingly, when I hide my true self from others, You already know the truth. And so here we are, my Lord, and I purpose to yield to You this day; may You mercifully and graciously help me follow and learn from You, embracing Your presence and directions concerning my life by faith.

The Chapters of Life

The End

Helper, Transformation, Jesus.

"When you get into a tight place, and everything goes against you, till it seems as though you could not hold on a minute longer, never give up then, for that is just the place and time that the tide will turn."

~*Harriet Beecher Stow*

Years ago, I read about the conception of Jesus in the Holy Bible and how, during her pregnancy, Mary, the mother of Jesus, went to visit her cousin Elisabeth. The Bible went on, in Luke 1:39-44, to say how Elisabeth was in her sixth month of pregnancy at the time of Mary's visitation. Furthermore, when Mary arrived and began to speak, the baby within Elisabeth began to leap, and she was filled with the Holy Spirit.

I realize there are many different beliefs and religions in the world. I mention this because I consider myself Christian and believe in God the Father, God the Son, and God the Holy Spirit.

I also believe the God I believe in does not make mistakes, and thus, every word of His has a purpose. As a result, I decided to dig deeper into the words within this passage of scriptures. In doing so, I thought about the various trimesters in a natural pregnancy, the first being a time of transition from fertilization to cells, along with implantation and the initial development of major body organs. The second involves weight gain and movement, the full development of organs, and a fetus's ability to hear, swallow, and kick. While the third, a time of maturity and delivery.

I intentionally paraphrased all that is involved in this *most amazing and miraculous* time, sharing just enough to introduce what was placed on my heart in hopes it may be of encouragement to you as it was to me. To begin with, I noticed when Jesus was developing in the first trimester, Elisabeth's child was ending development in the third and last trimesters. This reflection is worthy of pause to carefully note: *When Jesus was in His beginning stages, Elisabeth's child was in his ending term.* As I pondered this more, I thought about when I began to know Jesus for myself. I was in my early twenties and had finally realized the break-up between me and my daughter's father was for real and that our engagement was over and there would be no beautiful home with a white picket fence, an image that stood for a loving family and household in my mind at the time. The most heart-wrenching revelation, however, was coming to terms with how my daughter would not grow up in a house containing both her parents. I was devastated, not only because I was hurt beyond measure over the breakup, but because I never wanted to inflict even the tiniest bit of pain on my daughter. I thought I needed answers, but what I needed was instruction.

As I laid in bed worrying, I received a call out of the blue from one of my aunts, who happens to be a mighty prayer warrior and, for as far back as I can recall, exudes God with a fiery conviction. During the call, she encouraged me while simultaneously and empathetically acknowledging my pain and my tears. She then asked for permission to pray for me, which I granted. As she prayed, I felt hope enter my broken disposition. Before the call ended, she invited me to church, and afterward, when I say Sunday could not come fast enough, I mean Sunday could *not* come fast enough.

When I finally got to one of God's buildings, I began to see Him as Heavenly Father for myself, and just as I was concerned about my daughter, I realized He was just as concerned about me. His nature as love was further evident when He sacrificed His beloved son, Jesus Christ. As a parent, I know I could not have done this, for my human nature would be too weak to endure the pain of the process. Yet, from a spiritual perspective, I know the divine act was necessary to restore the sinful and broken nature of man back to a pure and unbroken God.

Such a sacrifice would require Jesus to be allured by human nature and desires throughout His time on earth while jointly upholding spiritual strengths. This exchange involved rejection, betrayal, false accusations, temptation, agony, and casualty, as well as excruciating pain, being "wounded for our transgressions" and "bruised for our iniquities" (*Isaiah 53:5*). I remember crying so heavily watching the movie "*The Passion of Christ*" which brought this moment of redemption to life so vividly. I felt like I was there, and I could relate to the time when Jesus [seemingly] felt forgotten by God as He hung on His cross pierced with outstretched arms, crying, "*My God, my God, why hast Thou forsaken me?*" *(Matthew 27:46)*. Keeping such a high ransom in mind, I thought about how, at any given moment, Jesus could have utilized the power within Himself to stop such suffering. And yet, He did not. Why? Because He understood His purpose and how "*God so loved the world, that He gave His only begotten Son, that whosoever believeth in Him should not perish, but have eternal life*" *(John: 3:16)*. What an amazing love, and how fitting of the power bestowed upon Jesus who manifested this love for us.

Ultimately, the death of Jesus, or should I say the end of His natural life on earth, resulted in victory and power over every turmoil He faced. As I studied this time, four lessons came to mind, which are parallel to the four lessons gleaned from the previous text. The first helped and continues to help me during some of my toughest battles. It stems from the realization that if

Jesus – a perfect being and the manifestation of God's word in the flesh – endured pain and suffering, so likely will I, or shall I say, *'we.'* At times, it may be inherent or undeserved, as was the case with Jesus. Other times, it may be the consequence(s) of a choice manifested per an action that we ourselves create. In either case, victory may come instantaneously; other times, you must work to overcome the battle as if your life depends on it because, well, it does. Kind of like the ultimate final stage of pregnancy, the delivery, where you must push past the pain to the manifestation of the promise.

The second lesson centers upon how *something within me also leaped* when I was introduced to the presence of Jesus, and in the exact moment of accepting Him into my being, I knew I was impregnated with something that was beyond me. From a spiritual position, this moment of conception is gender-neutral; thus, instead of a seed being planted within a natural womb, it is sewn into one's soul and spirit instead. The seed also grows like a natural fetus, except for it to grow, it must be nurtured and protected by the Word and Promises of God. As such, the more we stay connected to Him, the more we begin to sense His internal movement that triggers the need for a deliverance of sorts, hence the term rebirth.

The third lesson was not so immediate and was garnered from the child Elisabeth carried. In my opinion, this child was the first person that Jesus divinely influenced, apart from His earthly parents. This moment in time was activated the instant a divinely pregnant Mary encountered a destined-to-be pregnant Elisabeth. Each of these women were pregnant with purpose, but one could not manifest their purpose without an interconnectedness to the other. The child Elisabeth carried grew up and became known as John the Baptist. This is important to note because in biblical times especially, a person's name was extremely relevant. For example, the word Baptist is derived from the word baptize, which involves the activation of a belief. Accordingly, John more than lived up to his name, for he was the first to beckon for consideration to be born again. On the surface, this may seem impractical, but the critical distinction is how such a decision is within individual control as opposed to being the product of someone else's choice. Those who trusted in what John advocated were immersed with hope and expectation for this miraculous conversion fueled by a belief in Jesus, and it was his foresight that highlights what I would later come to understand. Such as how we sometimes deny ourselves someone or something good because we have not heard, believed, or experienced anything different. Instead, we may become captives to routine or targets of familiarity, sometimes without even realizing it.

The fourth revelation regards how Jesus only allowed certain individuals into His most intimate space during His time on earth. I realize the intent was so those chosen could not only get to know Jesus more personally, but also the God in Him. On the other hand, the carefulness of it all makes me think the significance of this structure goes a little deeper. The lesson to me being how important it is to be more selective regarding who and what we choose to invest in, as well as who we choose to allow into our personal space. We cannot be all things to all people, and sometimes, a choice must be made regarding who your inner circle should be and why. Of equivalent significance is that each of these individuals were carefully selected by God; and yet, when Jesus needed them most, they were not there for Him. In hindsight, I believe this was all part of God's perfect plan. But in foresight, these were individuals who were still challenged with humanistic traits. Thus, what greater way to display why we are not to idolize man but instead are so in need of a higher power and Savior. Jesus knew this, which I believe is why He also cried out on that same essential cross, *"Father, forgive them; for they know not what they do" (Luke 23:34)*. Yes, Jesus felt alone at times. But He also knew that man was not capable of providing what only God can give.

I end this section with a suggested expectation of what is to come, just as John the Baptist did. I state this because the next section will discuss my belief in why there is no longer a limit to who can dwell with Jesus, whom I wholeheartedly advocate as truly a most precious gift and presence. He is loving, gentle, and full of humility, and He sought - and still seeks — to bring love, peace, restoration, and healing amid hatred, chaos, and destruction.

Let Us Pray:

Father God, Thank You for the seed of Jesus. Thank You for paving a way out of the illnesses of society via the sacrifice of Christ at Calvary. It was there His blood was shed and became a lifeline to all who believe in Him and You. It was there He endured extreme pain and suffering as atonement for our sins that we might be born again. It was there that He cried, was tormented, and died...to self... It was there that He released the cares of this world and made way for another dimension of life with You. I pray You help us to grow deeply rooted in this union and all it entails, recognizing Jesus as the umbilical cord to true life and You as the source from which such life comes! Help us to breathe in this sustenance. Help us to see with spiritual vision. Help us to walk, and to talk, and to look more and more like a representation of You and not the image of our own corporeality. May our minds be renewed, and our child-like characteristics and tendencies shifted over time, growing through the parental guidance of You, our Heavenly Father, and Your Nature. May we be more willing to rest in Your presence and at the feet of Jesus. And as we are enabled to digest greater substances, may we be consumed by the essence of Your word and not just the formula our flesh craves during initial stages of development, albeit equivalent

importance. Lord, thank You for Your peace. Lord, thank
You for Your promises. Lord thank You for Your provisions,
patience, and protection as we purpose to navigate through
life and all that seeks to cultivate us. May You forever
overshadow all counterfeit things and beings as we
relinquish control and surrender to the process of
transforming and transitioning.

The Chapters of Life

NEW Beginnings

Comforter, Hope, The Holy Spirit.

"But the Comforter, which is the Holy Ghost, whom the Father will send in My name, He shall teach you all things, and bring all things to your remembrance, whatsoever I have said unto you."

~John 14:26

For there to be a new beginning, something must come to an end. In my encounters, I have learned very seldom do we experience something new without letting something go; or change, without allowing something to grow. I remember one evening when I pleaded with God all night for help in this area. Ironically, this was the day before Easter Sunday, so as I prepared to go to church the following morning, I couldn't help but think, what better day to expect change than on Resurrection Day! In other words, the day Christians honor Jesus for how He defeated death by rising above it literally and figuratively to reveal new life. In doing so, He simultaneously validated God's promise that we, too, can live again despite the pain of current circumstances.

Further, when Jesus rose to heavenly victory, He didn't leave the world without His presence but instead provided a way to have greater access to Him, which is through His Spirit.

Getting back to the day at hand, I was certain God heard my cries the previous night, but I was not at all prepared for what I was about to encounter. As I was driving to park my vehicle in the church parking lot, I abruptly came face-to-face with something I was struggling to accept. Everything, and everyone, had to be perfectly aligned for this chance encounter to occur, down to the seconds I left my home and the last-minute change to forego plans to pick up my daughter and meet her at church directly instead. I was beyond dismayed and knew manifestations of a splintered cross were piercing every fiber of my being in a most traumatic way. Initially, I put up a good smokescreen, but as the day went on, it felt like I was slowly disintegrating, as if my body and soul were engulfed with flames. On the one hand, I knew God was the answer to my blazing affliction. On the other hand, echoes of corrupt passions drove me toward the source of my despair, and the closer I got to this obscured reality, the deeper my wounds grew. Fatality began to knock on the door of my anguish, and not only did I answer this call of what felt like internal destruction, I entertained its company as well by allowing myself to dwell in the aftermath of agony, anxiety, and bewilderment.

As I was running out of breath, there was a presence within that helped fuel and propel me forward time and time again. This was key because in the natural realm we can typically be assured of periods of change; but in the spiritual realm, seasons tend to only shift once we exert the effort(s) required to be restored. I believe wounds from our past choke the life out of our present when we do not make this shift and that even unhealed families are divided for similar reasons, giving birth to the same nuclei, albeit through different generations, until reform occurs.

I later realized the fuel I sensed was that of the Holy Spirit. The Bible refers to the Holy Spirit as both comforter and counselor, the same as Jesus, but in a different form. Further, the word spirit means "the nonphysical part of a person which is the seat of emotions and character." It can be used interchangeably with life force, temperament, strength, resilience, and one of my most personal favorites, moral fiber. An excerpt from the bible reads, *"The spirit is willing, but the flesh is weak" (Matthew 26:41), and boy, was I in a weakened state with a* great need for a supernatural takeover. I was going downhill fast when I relied on my own strength; yet, simultaneously, especially in the moments I felt I couldn't hold on any longer, something greater than me would proclaim from within, "You can make it," "Keep going," and "this too shall pass." I later developed more of a willingness to apply pressure to the pain, putting my crutches aside and learning instead to walk on my broken heart and crawl through my wounded soul. The more I did, the more I began to face things head-on while concurrently loosening chains of bondage. I guess you could say I pressed past the distress of my mess to the message.

Around this time, I also recall a powerful revelation from a speaker at a work conference I attended. The speaker was Steven Gaffney, and he stated, "Time does not heal all wounds; time deepens the wound and the problem when left unresolved." After embarking on various journeys of healing and discovery, I could not agree more with this statement. It opened the eyes of my understanding in a way that persuaded me to take both ownership and initiative if I wanted to see a change in my life, to include being accountable for my own wrongdoings and not just grieving things I felt were wrongly done to me. My loved ones were also so instrumental in this battle. They helped ignite change through their love, support, and prayers, but I was still the one who had to allow the fiery process to consume me. As I did, the Holy Spirit was present to ensure the flames thereof did not annihilate me.

I pause here to meditate on the word *present*. This word can mean a gift or a physical presence, and the Holy Spirit is indicative of each. For example, when Jesus was physically on earth, there was limited space for people to be in His presence at once due to human constraints. But when Jesus departed from the earth, the

Holy Spirit was released in His stead. As such, despite how Jesus was no longer seen physically, His Holy Spirit remained present to fill all the spaces and places that He could not mobilize in human form. This space, first and foremost, includes our innermost being, and it is available to anyone wanting to have a more personal relationship with God the Father and Jesus the Son.

I first received the gift of this divine presence when my former pastor explained to do so only required that I believe, and then receive, just as you would do with someone handing you a gift. I learned I had to open not only my hands with expectation but my heart and mouth with desire and gratitude as well. Once I did, from that day forward, I was further and forever changed. Not because I was shielded from life's challenges, as I mentioned before. But because in the midst of said challenges, I know beyond doubt it was His Spirit that assured me I was not alone and that I was equipped to not only be a conqueror but even more than this.

There was also a third and fourth lesson I learned about the Holy Spirit. The third is intertwined with the promises of God. For God does not take back what is given. Instead, we may change, and life may change, but God, Jesus, and the Holy Spirit remain the same. They each have a different role, yet they are equally one, so much so that when God provided a permanent provision of restoration to Him through Jesus, He also accounted for a counselor, comforter, and guide to help maintain a relationship with Him.

The fourth lesson also involves being intertwined, but this time with Jesus. His spirit would often remind me the battle I faced was not physical, but more often the aftermath of a spiritual stronghold manifested. Accordingly, I believe Jesus was able to withstand trial and tribulation in His human form because His Spirit kept Him focused on an outcome greater than what was naturally seen. Our own battles are no different. For I completely understand when it is easier to blame a person or occurrence for the pain of our sorrows; however, when I view the same encounter from a spiritual perspective, I can sometimes link my harm to the seed of another person's trauma or to a symptom made from my own substances.

As I close this chapter, I dance in my spirit to a beautiful ballad by Bryan and Katie Torwalk entitled "Holy Spirit," which I often cry out to God while listening to. The song declares:

"There's nothing worth more. That will ever come close. Nothing can compare. You're our living hope. Your presence, Lord. I've tasted and seen. Of the sweetest of love. Where my heart becomes free. And my shame is undone. In Your presence, Lord. Holy Spirit, You are welcome here. Come flood this place and fill the atmosphere. Your glory, God, is what our hearts long for. To be overcome by Your presence, Lord."

Let Us Pray:

Holy Spirit. You truly are the melody behind the song of my heart... May You help me transition to the new beginning You have destined for me in a way that is healthy, undisguised, and wise, a way that is also unselfish to those who love and care for me, as well as to those who chose to pass me by. May You guide and instruct me as only You can, and as if we were a beautiful ballad brought to life through movement, may I sense Your presence, direction, and divine abilities as we dance. Today, I purpose to let go of depression, confusion, unforgiveness, loneliness, temptation, anger, rejection, fear, and/or (insert battle); and instead, I declare I am no longer indebted to what and who has held me captive causing me to gamble my soul and devalue my existence. I know these things can be overcome through the help of the Holy Spirit, the sacrifice of Jesus, and Your divine grace and provisions; thus, I thank You for being the light amid dark places, breathing new life within while freeing me from torment. You are a miracle worker, the ultimate counselor, and my greatest advocate; thank You for never giving up on me and for restoring healthy passions. I appreciate Your love, Your strength, and Your patience with me; thank You for never ignoring my call or need to be freed.

Introduction to

The Seasons of Life

Gardening Your Soul

The altering elements of seasons are pertinent mentally and emotionally just as much, if not more than they are applicable in natural environments. In other words, our thoughts, actions, and deeds are often the result of an established period in our lives, from lessons we may have learned growing up to various circumstances over time that contributed to the state of our current being.

The Seasons of Life

WINTER

"Sometimes God calms the storm. Sometimes He lets the storm rage and calms His child."

~*Leslie Gould*

When I think of winter, I think of cold weather, dryness that depletes moisture, and the higher frequency for dreary, ashen skies. I think about how marketplaces contain fewer items to select from, with some items more costly than usual because of weather restrictions and being out of prime growing season.

What winter also reminds me of, however, are traits and attributes related to periods that are hardest to endure. Examples of which can be gleaned from garments worn and actions taken when amid a chilling storm. Such as being clothed in layers we hope will keep us protected and warm, being similar to the notion of how we may wear coatings of depression and inner turmoil. Congruent to this is the hat or scarf we use to shield our head and face from bitter air, for during winter seasons, we can embody extreme sensitivity and become masked with deception if not careful. We may even trample in boots that are fitting for snow, yet in the conjectural sense, those same boots are unfit to tread into the depths of our souls. Not to mention times when it gets exceedingly frigid, such as times when we're a lot more willing to pay someone else to plow through what has become so rigid. Or if we do decide to dig around such conditions on our own, we may rush to reveal access points and miss what has grown. When we return indoors, perhaps we burn firewood for a cozier resting place, but in this analogy, our heart is the chimney, and it could be full of smoke we don't know how to properly release or embrace.

If you grew up as I did, windows may also be covered in plastic, thereby enabling another layer between us and the outdoors. I relate this correlation to how our pain and trauma often prevents others from getting too close to our core. Lastly is the gloominess of winter, which often emits the basis for less recreation and more sleep, and it is in this state of being we sometimes snooze for too long or, worse, hibernate with an enemy.

This rhetorical account of winter is, of course, my lyrical way of sharing experiences had during my wintry seasons. I was incredibly good at hiding what I was enduring until, one day, I ran out of reasons. My soul was by far diminished, and I didn't think I would ever make it out of such a darkened state. It followed me everywhere I went and made its presence known no matter the place.

Deep down, I knew there was something in me that was not supposed to perish, but I was so depressed all I could do was mourn my mistakes, disappointments, and regrets. I even recall once being awakened by an inner voice that said, *"Sabrina! STOP mourning your own life!"* It was the same voice that led to the writing of this book, and it is the same voice that still listens as much as it guides. Then, there was another instance that truly stood out because I completely stopped making efforts to better my situation. I even started planning my own memorial service, for I was overwhelmed with relentless tribulation.

I began writing letters to concerned loved ones, pinning precise details along with rationale for the pain that I was feeling, sharing how I had grown so very weak, distraught, and tired, with no more patience to wait on my healing. I remember one day, I was so full of distress that I collapsed in my daughter's arms and just cried and cried. I felt so guilty and pleaded for her forgiveness, trying my best to explain how I tried.

This battle with rejection, oppression, and discouragement lasted uninterrupted for several excruciating years. I honestly thought my story was over, yet I am still here. I may not be where I want to be, but I thank God I'm not where I was. He carried me through this most chilling downpour, and He used others to help give me sustenance. As He breathed new life within me, I eventually gained strength to begin crawling towards a better path; some days are still particularly challenging, however, the weight of death no longer holds me back.

Food For Thought:

In the words of Dr. Martin Luther King, Jr: *"If you can't fly, then run; if you can't run, then walk; if you can't walk, then crawl; but whatever you do, you have to keep moving forward."* This is one of my most favorite quotes. But I also believe when you are not stable enough to move, it is okay to merely be still and rest in God's arms of strength. I believe not only will He carry you, but that He will surround you with various forms of life support; filling your heart and soul with gentle whispers of reasons He does not want you to abort. May we also bear in mind how wintery conditions differ depending on where you dwell; as such, demonstrating unconditional love to those who may be in a different place than us, is a most beautiful example of grace that just may help someone else to get well. Like, with me, for example, it was family and friends that helped to restore my broken nature and heart; they could have disregarded the status of my being, but they didn't, and now - thanks to them and to God – I have a new start.

The Seasons of Life

SPRING

"The flower that blooms in adversity is the most rare and beautiful of all."

~*Walt Disney Company, Mulan*

There is so much I love about springtime, which is my favorite season: blossoming flowers, sunny skies, gentle breezes, and beautiful butterflies. Not to mention a warmer climate, filled with groomed gardens so full of color and vibrancy, along with various manifestations of growth and productivity. But as much as I love springtime, the morning's drive to work on this particular day of writing reminded me of a part of the season I dislike, and that is road construction, as well as traffic jams due to said construction.

Though I have the least bit of interest in this part of spring, I realize it's a necessary element, especially the cleanup of debris and hazardous road conditions that are often an aftermath of previous seasons. Such a time reminds me of unresolved feelings and emotions we sometimes transfer from day to day, month to month, and year to year, typically without even realizing it.

In more snowy states, cleanup efforts may include the filling in of the infamous pothole, which is a literal hole in the road that can cause a flat tire if not careful, causing even more of a delay while en route to one's destination. This very encounter happened to me once after a few coworkers and I left an office Christmas Party. I volunteered to drive, and thus felt so terrible I not only caused myself a delay, but the stranding of two others as well. They were gracious enough to experience this setback with me, and together, we went to the auto mechanic, where my car was submitted for service. About an hour or so later, we were back on the road to our initial destination, albeit via the use of temporary transportation.

During this bump in the road, I had the comfort of selfless coworkers who helped keep me encouraged. The period was also short-lived, unlike times I can recall when the effect was nowhere near as brief and the experience nowhere near as pleasant. Times when I not only impacted my own progress but that of others due to my instability during the process of being deconstructed and repaved.

In contrast is a part of spring which I am very fond of, and that is gardening. Over the years, I had the pleasure of planting flowers with my mom. We'd sometimes have the dreariestlooking flowers to plant, such that I couldn't tell if they were still alive or not because they were so flimsy and faint in color. For this reason, I would often try to plant the flowers close together, trying to camouflage the scarceness, but Mom would always say, "Give them more space; they will grow." I would still try to imbed them closer together, but she would insist regarding my need to include space. Eventually, I obliged, and to my surprise, the flowers all began to blossom so beautifully. In addition, the more we fed and watered them, the more they continued to flourish despite sometimes appearing lifeless because of the heat or hidden because of weeds.

This process reminds me of a concept I refer to as "gardening the soul," which includes a time of planting, sowing, and reaping but also a time to dig up some of what was planted previously. The comparison is not at all different from what is involved with natural cultivation, for, in either scenario, the process goes beyond the surface and into our soiled, innermost parts. It is an experience often unpleasant to embrace at first, but just as the flowers I planted with my mom required distance, time, and nurturing to fully blossom, this period can become one of the most beautiful manifestations of change.

As I meditated on this season, I noted how the same tears I shed in my wintry state were not as cold; thus, they were able to infuse and filter through the fallow grounds of my heart. I also started to address things that weighed me down and hindered my growth, things that kept me immobile and fixated on a place that was no longer productive. I began to think back to the stagnant period my wintry season alluded to, for there is generally no good growth during periods of stagnation, and my comfort zone blinded me from the decay that had developed within.

Such stagnation is comparable to the hidden ditch in the road, like the one I encountered when I hit that pothole. Yet, instead of an actual object of wear and tear, I was the target, tired and depleted because of pierced emotions and disappointments. Additionally, one of the most invaluable, and perhaps hardest, lessons I realized during this time was my need to detangle from certain individuals and circumstances comparable to weeds that can grow in the midst of a garden, triggering ruin if not plucked up.

If you ever find yourself in such an environment, I encourage you to give time, time, for I firmly believe when we are diligent to endure this season of our lives, healthy transformation will be revealed; however, we must allow ourselves both the space and patience necessary to grow. An example of this can be seen in the amaryllis, an amazing flower I first learned about when a coworker brought one of these precious gems into the office years ago. I would admire its beauty as I passed by my coworker's desk, and we eventually talked about their planting and preservation process. What captured my attention most was after the flower was no longer in its growing season, my coworker would take the bulb from the same flower and store it in the corner of the basement during the winter. They would then replant the same seed the following spring, where it would again bloom with just as much if not more, beauty and vibrancy.

I call the flower amazing because there were times I'd walk into the office and notice how the plant grew well over ten inches overnight, leaving me truly astonished. Of course, this growth was merely an outward reflection of internal development. In other words, a lesson to keep grooming what is on the inside, and instead of rushing the process or giving up, allowing the results to unfold more naturally.

I honestly don't know if I feel so fondly about this flower because of what I witnessed and discovered or because it reminds me so much of me. For instance, I, too, was thriving at one time in life. I was an ordained minister and was so thirsty for God. But then I grew stagnant because of layers of pain and discouragements I just could not bear anymore. I found myself buried in chilling surroundings, like the basement corner my coworker used to preserve the seed of the amaryllis. I also needed to be nourished back to life, especially during my last spiritual battle, where I, too, appeared lifeless because of ditches and gloom I got stuck in.

On the other hand, there were occasions I'd emerge from constructive periods to reveal more of my hidden treasures, for though I was weak, my base continued to be strong. However, let me be clear: this stability wasn't because of my ability; instead, it was because I learned to rely upon Jesus Christ, who is a firm foundation, which is something my mother also bestowed upon me. This prompted me to not only accept, but to also embrace, the symptoms of my broken nature, whereby I had to be restored and redeemed one tier, rather tear, at a time. In the Japanese culture, there is a tradition I absolutely love called "kintsugi," which conveys this inspiration perfectly. It involves the repair of broken pottery by mending the areas of rupture with a lacquer made of gold, silver, or platinum for the purpose of embracing imperfections and revealing the beauty of human flaws.

The last and final thought I venture to give in this section stems from a concept more relative to this book's title. I refer to it as the womb of Mother Nature, which I further interpret as an area of expansion that is extraordinarily deep beyond the earth's surface. In addition, when a seed is planted within the soil of her womb, it is germinated by waters produced by the ultimate Creator Himself, Father God. This germination may occur from water released from heavenly springs in the form of rain or through a well filtered from the temperament of immeasurable dew points. As the seed within her soil begins to grow, roots are formed. I call these umbilical cords to nature's life. Over time, the character of the seed starts to show in the form of outward appearances that are firmly affixed to what the eyes cannot see. If this exposure were to manifest as a tree, it has the potential to grow over 300 feet and live over 3,000 years, intertwining with other roots to develop incredible sustainability. I relate this to how we as individuals are limited to what we can achieve by ourselves, but when we link with others, greater grounds can be covered, and more lives can be impacted.

Food for Thought:

As seeds grow and as roots run deep, may we remember to pluck up the weeds. May we also be mindful of the bugs and drugs that can contaminate, so we in turn can exterminate, what has grown or is attempting to grow, evaluating our heart, and assessing what feeds our soul. Likewise, when we attach ourselves to different sources, may we remember the impact we seek. So, for example, if we want to produce love and good energy, may we connect to such sources as opposed to binding ourselves to who or what extinguishes life and vitality.

The Seasons of Life

SUMMER

"You took all my hurt away, warmed me up inside like a summer day."

~ Adapted from Destiny's Child, Heard a Word Lyrics

If I were to take a poll, I would bet on summer being the most preferred time of the year. It is a time of backyard barbeques, pool parties, and school breaks, along with a time of greater relaxation and the enjoyment of longer, sunnier days. The name itself means the warmest season of the year, which differs in temperature and duration depending on whether you live in the northern or southern hemisphere.

While writing this book, I moved to a warmer climate in pursuit of a *new season*. Ironically, the place I moved to is known as the "Sunshine State," and it was there I quickly learned – or rather was reminded – how *the state of one's being has more to do with conditions that are within as opposed to external environments.* To make this more personal, I literally dwelled amongst some of the most beautiful scenery full of palm trees and gorgeous sunsets, but I was unable to appreciate the views others longed for due to the acidic status of my emotions and transgressions. This became more evident whenever I went back to my hometown to visit. It didn't matter if I was greeted with below-freezing temperatures or the summer heat; my internal temperament remained the same, especially the closer I got to who and what triggered my move in the first place.

I remember growing ill during this one visit in particular, but not because of natural weather conditions. Instead, it was the disposition in my mind that went through a severe climate change, spinning with thoughts and feelings that felt like an inner hurricane. I needed care but was too ashamed to seek safety or adhere to sound advice. I remember wanting to go to sleep so badly I took an entire bottle of sleeping pills but still could not fall asleep, for the torment and pain was more awake.

In the days following, which included Christmas, I continued to have a beating heart, but my soul felt so lifeless. After this very emotional visit with my family, I flew back to *the Sunshine State* thinking I had the perfect opportunity to take my final rest, and I thought this because my daughter stayed behind for another week so no one had direct access to me. I made plans to time a message with the subject line 'send help,' which would automatically transmit to others so my daughter wouldn't be the one to find me *sleeping.* By this time, I researched my life insurance policy, and I knew enough funds were available to take care of bills, including my memorial service, which I planned with precise details down to what I wanted the room to look like, sound like, smell like, and feel like when others entered. I also knew what I'd wear, which was the dress I envisioned if I were ever to get married, for I was hoping despite my actions, I would still get to meet my bridegroom in heaven.

During this time, I had begun to also purchase keepsake gifts for my daughter and took measures to ensure her living and educational expenses would be covered, for she was still in college at the time. I then directed my efforts to not cause concern, so I started to reply to text messages from loved ones knowing the "I miss you too," the "I appreciate you," and the "I love you always and no matter what" replies were my cryptic way to say goodbyes. In return, I was flooded with messages letting me know I was being prayed for and that there was no need to apologize for not replying because when I went silent, is when 'they' prayed even more.

I began to remember my mother's heart-wrenching hug when I first moved and how her tears bathed my neck as she squeezed me ever so tight. I also recalled the look in my daughter's eyes when I found myself in the hospital; she was so scared, so worried. I thought these prayers must be working because my heart began to feel again, and I ended up pressing my way to church the following Sunday, which happened to be New Year's Day. I was too vulnerable and distraught to engage, but deep down, I knew how important it was to allow the power of God's words to hover and agree over me.

The message in service that day was about a birthing taking place and how, up to this point, the baby was being formed but had now crowned and was ready for delivery. How there would not only be a birthing but a simultaneous acceleration of growth. The pastor went on to reiterate the same story God used to minister to me years ago, as I wrote about in the previous chapter, down to how Jesus and John the Baptist were conceived only six months apart. As if this wasn't enough, the pastor further discussed *seasons* and how, when it comes to spiritual things, the timing is not dependent upon a calendar but when you receive the revelation needed to go to the next period. All I could do was think, "Okay, God. I am listening, and I know You are with me."

After service ended, I admittedly didn't leave completely transformed or anything close to this. Instead, another seed of hope was planted in my spirit, and I decided to give all of what I was feeling another day. From there, minute by minute, hour by hour, and day by day, my soul and spirit began to experience revival.

Food for Thought:

Spiritual and emotional battles don't change automatically. Likewise, internal temperaments require more than external climate change to adjust.

I wrote this chapter from a position of shame that has, and continues to be, healed from past conditions and trauma. I also write from a place of enduring humility and with a holy conviction, asking should you feel as I did during this exceptionally low point in my life that you will be still, and wait. Allow yourself to be saturated with and carried by the prayers of others, which I can attest are answered by the promises of God. The manifestation may not be instantaneous, but may you find comfort in knowing God's delays are not His denials. Sometimes, things do not change because He is merely waiting for us to learn a necessary element required in our next season. Other times, we know the answer but may not have the enablement to let go.

I guess that's why summer seasons are the hottest. We can become so exhausted from the heat until all that is left to attain is weariness from thirst. Should this apply to you, my prayer is for God to immerse you with His presence and drench you in His love and living waters like never before. Please also consider talking to someone you trust, a therapist, or even a national lifeline at 1-800-442-HOPE or 988.

The Seasons of Life

FALL

"When life knocks you down, you had better pick yourself up before you get kicked in the teeth."

~ *Author Known to God*

I was in my senior year of high school the first time I heard this quote. I don't recall which class or the instructor's name, but I was pregnant with my daughter at the time, and I remember thinking to myself, *"How silly of a statement."* Yet, here we are, over twenty years later, and this assertion remains embedded in my spirit, loudly ascending during different happenstances. I realize it is easier said than done to pick yourself up when you are down, so let me share with you a story about Wallie.

Wallie is a fighter. He's a squirrel that obtained this name after being trapped in my apartment wall before my first move out of state. Initially, Wallie would run around in my bedroom ceiling, but eventually, he landed inside the wall. I listened to Wallie scratch and claw at my walls for five straight days, as calls to management and the humane society didn't result in any action until day six. The observations that followed were both enlightening and inspiring. I hope you feel the same as I share more about this occurrence.

For starters, Wallie ran around in my most intimate place, my bedroom, and since he was in my bedroom ceiling, he was also in my *headspace*. He was constantly moving, constantly running, and constantly causing all kinds of havoc. This chaos by Wallie reminded me of the battlefield we may encounter in the bed of our mind, will, and emotions. For me, such a war manifested as thoughts of pain, destruction, and wonders of how, why, and whether my current state of being will ever cease. Further, once the running around stopped, it was not because Wallie was free, but it was because he became trapped, by a gap, he could not see. He then underwent what I termed *the fight of his life*, for I could hear his efforts to break free only to keep falling again and again and again. Interestingly enough, Wallie would only make noises when I was home alone. Thus, when maintenance and pest control came to investigate the 'unbearable' sounds I complained about, others would likely not even believe Wallie existed had I not thought to record what I was hearing.

But Wallie did exist, and together, we established a routine – familiarity centered in fear, discouragement trapped by desperation, and loneliness embraced by a lack of self-love. Once I began to put a name to what I was hearing, I began to speak back. "Wallie!" I would say. "You have got to make these noises when others are here to help because I cannot get you out of there. Wallie! I don't want you to give up, so keep fighting. Wallie! I admire your fight. Wallie! You're teaching me to not quit. Wallie! You're teaching me to keep pressing on. Wallie! How on earth are you still alive without any food to eat or water to drink? Wallie! Don't you give up! Wallie! I am doing all that I can to get you out of there… Wallie! Please don't die on me, as I know what it's like to be tormented by thoughts of dying alone. Wallie! Please don't give up on me. Wallie. Wallie! WALLIE!! *Are you still there?*"

Day after day, night after night, Wallie's fight grew more and more faint, and the piercing sounds of desperation I heard before became mere whispers of less fight, less hope, less and less life. I grew so saddened once the silence grew louder, and I began to think Wallie was no longer alive. But then, ever so often, I would hear a faint reminder letting me know he was still there. Still trapped. Still trying. Still breathing. Yet seeming to be surrendering. When the walls were finally vetted into, thanks to the use of infrared lighting, I got a call while I was at work to let me know Wallie was taken out of his darkened state. To my surprise, he was also still alive, but with a surprising twist. For trapped within my walls were not one, but two of his kind, and sadly, one of the two did not make it. I begin to view this turn of events in a different light. Did Wallie have a companion during his or their battle to break free, or was he merely battling with himself?

Before the call ended, and in true concern, I asked, "What will happen to the two now?" To which I was answered, "One will roam free in the land of infinite possibilities, while the other would be buried." What a thought-provoking response, I pondered. For even when the battle we fight is within ourselves, there are parts of us that must die so that other parts can live. Of even greater significance is how the decision regarding what part remains and what part perishes is all our own. It makes me wonder if that were true for Wallie, what part of him lived, and what part of him was buried?

Food for Thought:

There is a scripture that says God uses the foolish things of the world to confound the wise. Translation – A squirrel, trapped within my wall for five nights and six days, planted a seed of encouragement in my heart, soul, and spirit. A seed to keep fighting until I'm free and can see the light of day. Some days are still harder than others. Yet, I am encouraged knowing God promises never to leave us alone in battle or any other time in our lives. Sometimes, I may fall. Sometimes, I may grow tired. Other times, I merely need to surrender so that my Lord and Savior can come in as the great hero that He is to rescue and set me free. I don't believe the number of days and nights Wallie was trapped are coincidental, for five is the number of *Grace,* which God so freely offers, and six is the number of *'man'* who has been given freewill to choose which paths in life to take.

Closing

When it was first placed on my heart and in my spirit that my journaled thoughts would one day be a book, I honestly didn't believe it. However, over the years, there were promptings along the way instructing and encouraging me to write. The chapters were all solidified the first time I journaled, but the content, my God – it has been years in the making and continues to be an ongoing story.

For this reason, I decided to take the four chapters I was inspired to write and split them into part one and part two. I did this because I believe part one is the story I am overdue to release, both literally and figuratively, whereas part two is the story I, in so many ways, am still composing as my life's journey continues to evolve and unfold.

As I venture into my next chapter, my hope is that we each develop the elements necessary to overcome seasons that are not healthy for us, and that we also will not camouflage the condition of our inner selves when help is needed. I'm also an avid believer that, just like with natural seeds and plants, spiritual and soul roots grow deeper over time and can either be nourished with life-giving nutrients, such as water, sun, and positive light, or with the contrary, such as anger, resentment, or strife. Should we continue to allow the latter to grow, counterfeit plants will harvest as opposed to a flow of healthy nourishment that is crucial to our overall wellbeing.

Lastly, as I conclude the final prayer of this particular text, I want to encourage you to read two letters I have written in honor of my farewell to the past. The first is a letter that contains things I wished to tell another but couldn't. The second is a letter that contains the things I often told to others but not to myself.

Thank you again so much for indulging me; I appreciate it, and *you* deeply.

~*Sabrina Nichole/aka Bri*

Closing Prayer

*Most Gracious and Heavenly Father. I come to You in the
authenticity of this moment, desperate for You, longing for
You, apologetic to You for the idols I worshiped in Your
place. I am so deeply sorry, and I thank You for loving me
beyond my flaws, weaknesses, and mistakes. I need Your
strength, Heavenly Father. I cannot make this journey
through life without You. My soul is starved, my spirit so
famished. Please water me with the oil of Your anointing and
heal my mind, body, will, and emotions as only You can do.
Please take away the hurt and allow only the revelation of
this process to grow. Please mold, fix, and/or replace the
areas that are broken. Please allow me to rest in Your peace.
Please allow me to stand via Your strength, embraced by
Your grace when I am weak. Please shelter me from all hurt,
harm, and danger. Please cover me from the storm and
minister to my wounded heart via Your angels and Heavenly
Nature. Please bless those who kept me lifted up when life
kept me down. Please allow me to hear the melodies of Your
most merciful and miraculous sound. May my worries, cares,
and distresses be laid to rest. While my heart goes on to beat
for You via the awe of Your majestic peace, healing, and
holiness.*

Letters to My Past

Dear YOU

I am in so much pain. I especially write this letter in hopes of a good response because, truthfully, it's you that I blame.

For my tears, my broken heart, and pierced soul. Never in my wildest dreams did I ever think you could be so bold.

Why did you lie? Why did you leave? What exactly did I do wrong that caused you to reject and ghost me?

The very fiber of my being was so, so into you. Went to bed with you on my mind; woke up in a similar state. How is it that such a beautiful feeling could turn into what feels like hate? That might actually be too strong of a word. Though if hate is the opposite of love, then maybe not. How did you even get here in the first place? How were you able to creep into this spot?

I was clearly wrong about us, or maybe I wasn't, but some things just aren't meant to be. My former pastor used to often say," The right thing at the wrong time is still the wrong thing."

Nonetheless, this pain in my chest keeps resurrecting time and time again. And just when I think I'm over you, I'm met with a reminder of your touch, your laugh, your grin.

I talked to God about it. Told Him I know He loves you as much as He loves me. Asked Him to help me to let go once and for all. Because this burden is too hard and heavy for me to carry.

He told me to stop giving you to Him and then taking you and the situation-ship back! Told me in order to heal, I had to come to terms with this new reality I didn't want to accept.

Cause no matter what went wrong, right, or indifferent between you and me. I have been shackled to something that no longer exists, which only God has the keys to free.

As I talked to Him more and more. He began to reveal more about myself as well. I was reminded how I am far from perfect. And could have very well helped to enable that hell cell where I dwelled.

So, for my part in all, I apologize and ask for forgiveness. And should we never talk again, it's all good because God has been there for me in ways you never can be and has mended my brokenness.

Grace, Peace & Love to you!!

Dear ME

Hey Gyrl, Hey. I need you to stop tripping. Be kind and gentle towards yourself, and remember, life is worth living. Also, pause, breathe, and release because we all make mistakes. Take more moments to immerse yourself in the gift of Father God's mercy and grace.

Ima need you to keep treating others like you want to be treated, too, as opposed to how you were treated. So don't give him, her, or them your power anymore sis, and don't try to get even.

Instead, when emotions rage and feelings soar. Get on your knees and knock on heaven's door. Father God is there waiting to listen and talk, waiting to heal, strengthen, and guide. But you gotta humble yourself and trust the process, sis; let go of unforgiveness, guilt, shame, or pride.

Cause see, those are the adversary tactics, whose intent is to confuse, kill, steal, and destroy. He wants to rob you of your peace and to annihilate your joy.

But let's declare today baby girl, we gone leave the past in the past once and for all. Yeah, you may stumble or error again, but now you know how to overcome a fall.

You've also endured the chaos that can come with winter, spring, and summer seasons, too. But through it all, you now know for yourself that God has truly got you, boo!!!!

There were some lessons needing to be learned, some trauma to overcome. But rest assured, honey bunny, you are a victor and not a victim.

So, hold your head up high, and declare I made it!! Proclaim you're entering a new season full of peace, prosperity, favor, and divine enablement!

Ima need you to stay present, too, sis, and embrace the gift of now. Yes, wisdom says, plan for your future; but don't dwell so much on what maybe, could possibly, happen on tomorrows.

Cause truth is none of us can say with certainty what tomorrow will bring. But what I do know about tomorrow is that God will be the same, and if you let Him, sis, He will continue to get you through any and everything!!

So be encouraged, my dear girlsisterfriend, and know you've got this!!! Do more of what you love and less of what doesn't bring you happiness!

I'm rooting for you always, too, boo; remember the diamond that you are! For you are sealed by the blood of Jesus, with platinum status from all that fire you've overcome.

Recommended References

The Names and a Study of God
https://www.blueletterbible.org/study/misc/name_god.cfm
https://www.blueletterbible.org/search/dictionary/viewtopic.cfm?topic=IT0003853

The Names and a Study of Jesus
https://www.blueletterbible.org/study/parallel/paral19.cfm

The Names and a Study of the Holy Spirit
https://www.blueletterbible.org/search/dictionary/viewtopic.cfm?topic=TT0000571

Numbers in Scripture
http://www.biblebelievers.org.au/number01.htm

You Say, God Says
https://reneeswope.com/wp-content/uploads/2013/05/Chapter-12.-WhatGodSays_31Promises.Printable.pdf

50 Biblical Affirmations that Will Change Your Life
https://gabbyabigaill.com/50-biblical-affirmations-that-will-change-your-life/

50 Best Positive Affirmations to Improve Your Mindset
https://gabbyabigaill.com/50-best-positive-affirmations-to-improve-your-mindset/

The Cocoon
http://wonderopolis.org/wonder/what-goes-on-inside-a-cocoon

Made in United States
Orlando, FL
06 May 2024

46564545R00049